Kris Jenner

A Kris Jenner Biography

Lotti Davidson

Table of Contents

Introduction

In July 2018, the iconic *Forbes* Magazine placed on its cover, a 21-year-old young woman on the verge of becoming "*the youngest-ever self-made billionaire*." The badge, "self-made," is one held in awe by many Americans raised on the national ethos of meritocracy, and having opportunities to maximize one's potential in order to pursue happiness. Americans tended to expect singular talent, grit and daring, of people lifting themselves up from wherever they came from. These were the prerequisites before one could earn the honor of being labeled "self-made."

Many of them were not expecting – nor accepting of - Ms. Kylie Jenner.

Already born to privilege and bearing a famous last name, she had a good and loving home and attended an exclusive private school (before shifting to homeschooling) where she was a cheerleader – already considerable privileges even *before* her beautiful, blended family starred in a hit reality show. She was only around 10 years old when *Keeping Up With the Kardashians* hit the airwaves in 2007, and as of this writing in 2018, is still running, on top of having spawned nine spin-off shows… one of which belonged to Kylie alone – *Life of Kylie*.

As if the rich couldn't get any richer, the show brought the tween fresh opportunities aplenty. She, sometimes alone and other times in various combinations with her family, lent their names and faces to clothing lines, nail polish, apps, even young adult dystopian fiction. They made money seemingly from everything, especially the lifestyle and image they depicted of themselves on social media. Eventually she was able to channel her fame and social influence into Kylie Cosmetics, a make-up line initially anchored on lip-kits that has since expanded and taken the beauty industry by storm.

Her success was not questionable. Her "self-made" badge, however, faced a lot of heated backlash. To call her "self-made," pointed out many an irate netizen, was to ignore the head-start accorded by her privileges, and cultivates a negative impression of the country's poorer sectors of society. It makes others appear lazier and less motivated when the truth was, they had structurally less opportunities. Even Dictionary.com had a say, tweeting, admittedly cleverly, a definition of "self-made" as "*having succeeded in life unaided*" with "*Used in a sentence: Forbes says that Kylie Jenner is a self-made woman.*" The tweet was a hit itself of course, because that is just what the Kardashians do. They stir the pot and create conversations.

Whether or not Kylie Jenner deserves the title of being "self-made" is debatable. Certainly, her siblings – who pretty much had the same opportunities as she – were not able to channel the same privileges into a business estimated to be worth $800 million and a personal net worth totaling an estimated $900 million. Not that any of them is a slouch; each and every Kardashian-Jenner sibling is worth upwards of $10 million dollars individually, because though it opens with her, this book is not about Kylie Jenner.

This book is about the underlying force powering her moves, and the moves of all her siblings. It's about the greatest edge of them all – having a mom like Kris Kardashian Jenner on your corner.

Because those who would begrudge Kylie Jenner's "self-made" badge would probably not deny it of her mother, formerly Kris Houghton of San Diego – high school graduate from a broken family with an allegedly alcoholic father. Now estimated to be worth $60 million on her own right, she is instrumental in the building and maintaining of her children's myriad careers. If people still have a hard time taking the Kardashians – and Kris – seriously, *Forbes* Magazine's Kylie Jenner feature and her $1 billion-ish estimated net worth should be the ultimate wakeup call. Indeed, one of the biggest 'family-owned businesses' in America and one of the most recognizable brands in the world is helmed by Kris, who theoretically on paper, has little to offer. But she is the chief architect and protector of the Kardashian brand, and the family business is the monetization, maintenance and yes, perhaps the manipulation and constant re-definition of modern-day fame.

Kris is their founder, CEO, COO and perhaps even the janitorial services of this diversified super-company – she is often the first phone call when members of the famous family inevitably finds his or herself in some sort of personal or professional trouble, and she is almost always able to clean up the mess and pick up the pieces. Sometimes the mess is a bad PR move. Other times, the pieces are that of her crying, broken children. Because beyond any other title she may have, Kris has shown herself to be a devoted mother. Unafraid to show affection, always effusive in her praise, never shy with her pride. She pushes when needed, pulls back and steps away when that is what is required. Watching her, one feels both embarrassment and endearment. She is probably the most humanizing face of a famous family whose existence is all-too-often detached from normalcy.

This is Kris Houghton Kardashian Jenner, or whatever incarnation she chooses to go by these days. With everything she has achieved, she could be anything. But before she got here she was Kris Houghton, beautiful teen from a broken family, on the lookout for a better life and seeing it linked to securing a good husband. She was Mrs. Robert Kardashian, high school graduate suddenly swept off her feet and into the halls of the powerful, popular and wealthy – and expected to play the part of Beverly Hills homemaker to the hilt. She was Mrs. Bruce Jenner, finally able to spread her wings and explore her heretofore undiscovered talents of managing a brand and a business. She was the former Mrs. Caitlyn Jenner too, from when her husband transitioned to a woman and she consequently had to weather the storms as gracefully as possible, before the cruel glare of the spotlight and the public eye. She now holds pride in her main role of mom and manager - "momager" – to her Kardashian and Jenner children, through five of whom, she is also a loving and indulgent grandmother.

This is Kris Houghton Kardashian Jenner – SELF-MADE - and all the she had made of herself, by herself.

I. Kris Houghton – The Early Years

Kristen Mary Houghton was born on the 5th of November, 1955 in San Diego, California, first of two daughters by her mother, Mary Jo Campbell and her father, Robert True Houghton. The young beauty was said to have mixed Dutch, English, German, Irish and Scottish roots along her family tree.

The union with Robert was not Mary Jo's – who is also lovingly known as "M.J." - first marriage. The tall, lithe, Arkansas native was born in 1934 and attended the charm school, Fashionality, when she was 15 years old. M.J. put her sense of style to good use and became a model, not to mention a retail clothing store owner later in her life. She wed her first kiss and high school sweetheart, who at that point she had been dating for four years, when she was only 18. This first marriage, however, did not stick – they divorced after two months (thus beating her infamous grandchild Kim's 72-day marriage to Kris Humphries decades later!). M.J. was 20 years old when she had her first daughter, Kris, who would be followed a few years later by younger sister, Karen.

Robert was an engineer and the Houghton family was middle-class, but Kris' parents' roughly decade-long relationship was tumultuous. Robert has been described as verbally abusive and had issues with alcohol. When the marriage ended, the divorce filing cited his cruelty. Kris' parents divorced when she was only 7 years old, but by some reports, Robert and M.J. may have split as early as when Kris was only 4. Either way, it was a rocky marriage and it ended with Mary Jo having custody of Kris and Karen. Their grandmother, Lou Ethyl Wyatt Campbell, had a hand in raising them too. Robert Houghton wouldn't be a very big part of his daughters' lives afterwards. He died in 1975 from a car accident. It's been reported that he and Kris reconnected not long before that at least, when she was 18 years old. Unfortunately, she allegedly saw for herself how severe her troubled father's personality could be.

Post-divorce, life moved on for the Houghton girls and their mom, Mary Jo. Shortly after Robert's exit, young Kris was discovered to have a cancerous bone tumor at the age of 8. It was severe enough that she required surgery, and there was even a risk of her losing her leg if it was discovered to have spread. Thankfully, she was successfully treated and eventually declared cancer-free, going on to recover with no problems.

As for Mary Jo, she found love anew. She married a businessman named Harry Shannon. The new family moved away from San Diego and tried to plant roots in Oxnard, California. It would, however, be a short stay; business problems would force the family back to San Diego after just a few months away. The newly minted Mary Jo Shannon's second marriage was not off to the best start, but she and Harry ended up staying together for 40 years, until his death from a 2003 car crash.

The stylish, entrepreneurial and hardworking M.J. may have been the original workaholic 'Kardashian' girl. Even when her daughter Kris and grandchildren rose to the top of modern celebrity, she kept working. She had been in retail for over 50 years, and had run a number of stores over her career. She founded Shannon & Co. Children's Boutique in 1980, a small store carrying kid's clothing and miscellany, situated in the low-key, beach town of La Jolla. Kris is said to have done her share of the work here and Kim, whose beautiful childhood photo hangs in one of the walls, is said to have spent some of her grown-up years helping out too, counting money on the floor. When the Kardashian sisters, Kourtney, Kim and Khloe opened up their store, DASH, in 2006, they were in many ways echoing the entrepreneurial spirit of the Campbell women; not just M.J., but also M.J.'s mom, Ethyl. Ethyl had a candle store where Kris worked when she was young. She was wrapping purchases, but also learning the ropes of running a business. M.J. eventually had a store too, so did Kris, and eventually, the three

Kardashian ladies of reality TV. Thus, over several generations, from Ethyl to MJ and from MJ to Kris and from Kris to her three Kardashian daughters – all these strong, independent women from the same family founded and maintained small businesses of their own.

The ultra-chic M.J. is often spotted out shopping with the girls (or on their and brother Rob's social media accounts, where she is often celebrated), and is a frequent presence in the family's hit TV show. She had grappled with cancer but is staying active well into her 80's. She is well-loved by her Kardashian-Jenner grandchildren; Kylie has a tattoo of her grandmother's name on her arm and had named a shade of lipstick in her honor; and Kim had used her as a model for her KKW collection of concealers.

These tributes from her multi-millionaire grandkids however, were still a long ways away from when M.J. moved back to San Diego with her new husband and her two daughters. Harry Shannon had a good relationship with his step-daughters and his death from a car crash in 2003 has been described by Kris as "*devastating*" to the family. He was a beloved father-figure to Kris. Good relationships aside, providing for a family was still not easy. And as Kris grew up, her complex family history and the myriad domestic and financial troubles they suffered are said to be among the reasons why she eventually became the woman that she is now – a woman of ambition, unbelievable work ethic and of course, a loving daughter, mother and grandmother. Apparently burdened by examples she had seen in her youth, early on she understood the benefits of a secure home and marriage with a good provider.

In San Diego, Kris attended Clairemont High School. Some of her peers revealed education did not seem to be her priority, but neither were high school boys. When she was 12, she volunteered at the school office. As a teenager, she worked at a donut shop. She also worked in her grandmother Ethyl's store, and later, her mother M.J.'s. Even from a young age, she seemed very interested in making money and working. In later interviews, she would credit her early work experiences as pivotal in learning not just about the nuts and bolts of a business, but also the values of responsibility, punctuality and professionalism, on top of deriving personal satisfaction from earning one's own money.

She may have found other means with which to attain the finer things in life aside from working, however… for after high school, the young stunner (who shared a resemblance with the actress Natalie Wood) would be found in the arms of popular, powerful and wealthy men who were at least several years older than her.

Romantic Conquests. What accounts for the shift from hard-working teen with no interest in boys to young seductress is unknown; some people have credited her mother, M.J., for teaching her how to charm men of means. Other critics would be more severe, calling M.J. an enabler and one even going so far as to liken M.J.'s actions with 'pimping out' her daughter. There is no proof of any of these allegations; perhaps M.J. was just unconventionally liberal in her daughter's upbringing. She, for example, had divorced twice at a time when it was taboo, and had always been a strong woman and independent thinker. She is even reportedly open-minded about her now-famous granddaughters' penchants for posing provocatively in photographs.

Aside from her mother, M.J., young Kris was also in the influential sphere of an older student, a popular cheerleader by the name of Debbie Mungle. Debbie, at the time an aspiring model who was heavily into the disco scene, has been described as fun, friendly and vivacious. She and Kris were said to be so close they were almost sisters.

Alfred M. Garcia. It was reportedly through Debbie that Kris met her first professional boyfriend, Alfred M. Garcia. Debbie, as was earlier mentioned, was an aspiring model and Garcia was a photographer, with credentials including a stint as posing instructor at Barbizon School of Modeling. He and Kris dated around 1972 to 1973. At the time, she was said to be a clerk at a woman's clothing store in a San Diego mall. He would later be quoted by the media as describing Kris' beauty, friendliness and attentiveness as a girlfriend, but also her drive for wanting better things in life. They broke up – he was focused on his career and she wanted other things, and perhaps it just did not work – but they remained friends, as proven by her tapping his photography services later in their lives.

After Kris graduated from high school, she and her good friend Debbie flew to Hawaii in 1973. It was reportedly a graduation present from M.J. There, when Kris was 17 and fresh out of high school, she is said to have met and quickly made another conquest: the handsome, Mexican-American professional golfer, Cesar Sanudo.

Cesar Sanduo. Cesar Sanudo, 11 years Kris' senior and aged 28 at the time, initially may have been unaware that he had picked up a teenager. Either way, the romance flourished for a while. Part of Sanudo's work was traveling for tournaments, and Kris followed him along in support. In the times she was not with him, he allowed her to stay at his townhouse in San Diego. By many accounts, Sanudo was serious about the relationship and wanted to marry her. According to some reports, he popped the question when she turned 19 and she had said yes, not that the engagement – if it did occur – would bring them down the aisle.

Cesar brought Kris to fancy events and introduced her to powerful people, letting her maneuver around the privileged world he moved in as a professional athlete. But she was a young, smart, charming and profoundly attractive woman who managed to cultivate other eligible options aside from her then-boyfriend, who grew more and more suspicious of her behavior. She was vivacious and flirtatious, and would even act upon her romantic impulses with at least one very prominent man – the powerful attorney and businessman, Robert Kardashian.

While Sanudo was away on a tournament, Kris went on a date with the persistent Kardashian and brought him home – to Sanudo's home that is, where they were reportedly caught in bed by the justifiably enraged pro-golfer. The cheating did not immediately result in a split, but the relationship soured quickly afterwards.

Robert Kardashian. Robert Kardashian was a catch in Beverly Hills in the 1970s. The Armenian-American, born in 1944, was also over a decade older than Kris like her pro-golfer boyfriend (and perhaps one-time fiancé), Cesar. Age was not at all a deterrent then and neither was Kardashian's relatively short stature. He was 5'8" (short enough that he is said to have worn shoes with lifts when he married Kris in 1978, while she wore flats!) and had a streak of white hair, but he was otherwise good looking and certainly had plenty of other charms. He hailed from a wealthy family that owned a multi-million-dollar meatpacking company, one of California's biggest for a time (it would eventually fall into scandal, but it would neither tarnish nor even touch Robert himself). In his own right, he was also a lawyer and businessman with a taste for – and enviable access to – the finer things in life.

Robert and Kris met at a horse racing track shortly after she took up with Sanudo, sometime around the spring of 1973. They forged a quick connection due to his persistence; she was reportedly hesitant to give him her contact details, but in the typical Kardashian style of never saying die, he is said to have found it through his connections. They became friends and later, more. Counter to this reported persistence, however, Robert is said to have actually been more in love with someone else than he was with Kris. Kardashian was said to have been head-over-heels for *the* Elvis Presley's gorgeous ex-wife, Priscilla at the time. Besides, if Robert's seniority was not an issue for Kris, *he* may have found the teenager too young to let the relationship go very far. Kris was so young when they met that she couldn't even bet at the racetracks. She was there supposedly because her mother M.J. went, but she had to be more of a spectator on the sidelines, where she ended up meeting the man she considered to be her first real love, Robert. At any rate the initial romance did not get very far on this first round. Kris was still somewhat committed to Sanudo, and Robert still had a fighting chance with the King's ex-wife.

There are varying accounts of how serious Priscilla Presley was about Kardashian. Some say the worldly beauty who moved in the King's circles refined Kardashian's tastes and in a sense "groomed" him. Others say she took up with Kardashian only because she had no better options at the time. Others yet say it was Kardashian who had lofty standards, and Priscilla tried her best to be more of the traditional Armenian-type housewife as he wished her to be. And then there are those that say that for Priscilla, no one would ever match her famously brilliant but troubled ex-husband, Elvis. Either way, whatever they had between them was fated for an ending.

In the meantime, in the less rarified world of Kris Houghton, it was time to recalibrate and find other means of attaining her dreams. At the age of 20, she became a junior flight attendant for American Airlines. She was reportedly attracted to the active and more social lifestyle of a stewardess versus that of her previous work as a store clerk. After all, being one would bring her more exposure to the larger world – and the sophisticated jet set who tended to take to the friendly skies in the late-1970s.

Some of the people who knew her at this time would speak of how stunning she was - tall, always impeccably attired, with a presence that could light up a room. By one former colleague's remembrances, Kris Houghton literally turned heads when she walked by at the airport. She tried to put that appeal into productive use. In 1977, she asked her ex-beau, Alfred M. Garcia, to take photographs of her in various attires (the pictures would be made public decades later and she looked young, fresh and beautiful in the black and white images), hoping the shots would lead her into a modeling career. While that ambition did not quite pan out, she did have other fish to fry.

Kris Houghton, stewardess, was often in the company of people with power and money. There are even stories of her being spotted driving fancy, apparently borrowed cars she could not have been able to afford on a junior flight attendant's salary. She always had grand goals, and one of the things she wanted most was Robert Kardashian. She wanted him back, and was willing to do everything in her power to secure him, especially after his romance with Priscilla Presley ended for good.

Kris trained as a stewardess for American Airlines in Dallas, and was eventually based in New York City – on the other side of the country from where Kardashian lived in Los Angeles. But she reportedly burned the phone lines calling him often, and even flew to and from Los Angeles frequently in a bid to win him back. She was eventually transferred to LA, and they were able to pursue their relationship in earnest.

The first of Kris Houghton's major life goals was achieved when the couple married in July of 1978. It was a lavish ceremony with all the proper trappings expected of a man of Robert Kardashian's stature. They honeymooned in Europe afterwards.

At the age of 22, Kris had secured for herself a husband, one of Beverly Hill's most eligible bachelors – a handsome, accomplished lawyer and businessman, scion of a wealthy family, and a devout born-again Christian with traditional values, to boot.

Kris Houghton, high school graduate, former store clerk and AA stewardess, exited the scene in a swirl of fancy white wedding lace, swept off her feet and into the Beverly Hills life by her high-flying new husband.

Mrs. Kris Kardashian had just stepped into the big leagues.

II. Mrs. Robert Kardashian

On the 8th of July, 1978, 22-year old Kris Houghton became Kris Kardashian via her marriage to successful lawyer and businessman, Robert Kardashian, who was more than a decade her senior. Their wedding was a lavish affair held at the prominent Westwood United Methodist Church, right in the heart of Westwood. The wedding venue as well as that of the reception, held at the prestigious (and pricey) Bel-Air Country Club, were in some ways a statement – the Kardashians were positioned to be major players in their fancy community. It shouldn't have been anything new to Robert; but the high school-educated, much younger Kris had a lot to learn if she were to navigate her new environs expertly.

The pair had reportedly known each other since Kris was only 17 and had other relationships before their winding roads met again in Los Angeles. Before they married, she moved into his fancy Beverly Hills home, but had no access to his extensive funds. Robert, who had come from entrepreneurial and hardy Armenian immigrant stock, wanted his young girlfriend to have a greater sense of the value of earned money.

The Kardashian Family Legacy. Robert Kardashian was said to be very proud of his Armenian roots (a sense he managed to imbue into his children, who would be outspoken in their Armenian advocacies after they became famous). When his family history was made public decades later (thanks to reports made primarily by the *Daily Mail*), he certainly seemed to have cause to be.

Armenia, a small country currently of some 3 million people, is bordered by territories that have at some point or another, had expansionist ambitions. Thus, along the course of Armenia's thousands of years of history (it is a very old civilization, and is amongst the earliest Christian ones), its myriad parts had been under the Ottoman Empire (via Turkey), The Persian Empire (via Iran), the Russian Empire, and when that fell, Soviet Russia too.

The Kardashians were known as Kardaschoffs (following the Russian style) in a part of Armenia under the Russian Empire. Belonging to a religious sect different from the Orthodox, they were subject to harassment that had them relocating to a different part of the country, Karakale. There, they were able to practice more freely and be amongst people who also shared their beliefs. Their religious affiliation as Molokans – who were not averse to believing in prophecy - became pivotal to their survival in the world-altering events that would follow the family's relocation.

In the 1850s, an illiterate 11-year-old boy made an unlikely prophet; he saw an apocalyptic vision of war, bloodshed, and a great journey over the seas. Years later, he would reiterate these prophesies and be instrumental in the move of many in their community. Those who believed, left Armenia quickly. Those who did not, stayed. And of those who stayed, it's been said, many perished from a series of catastrophic events… For while the young diviner was specific enough to point his people where to go –

toward the West Coast of the United States – few could have imagined the atrocities that those who stayed behind would suffer.

Part of Armenia had also been under the Ottoman Empire, which was in decline by the late 19th century while the Great Powers of Europe were on the rise. Russia was particularly threatening, and had even gone on to claim some contested territory. The Ottoman Empire was also feeling insecure due to rising nationalism amongst its subject states, which included Armenians who had stirrings of a desire for independence after centuries of Ottoman restrictions and being considered second-class citizens.

These insecurities quickly eroded the trust between the Ottomans and the Armenians. As the basic logic went, between the Russians and the Ottomans, the Armenians may side with the former, with which they shared religion, but also because with an Ottoman defeat, they may be able to hope for independence.

Armenians stated being deported in conflict areas as a precautionary measure. While this already raised concerns amongst Armenians as well as the international community, it wasn't long before things got worse. Systemic violence (the Turkish government still denies labels of "genocide" more than 100 years after the horrendous events) against Armenians started and really came to a head around 1915, when the Armenian Genocide is said to have started.

At the outbreak of World War I (where Ottoman Turkey sided with Germany and Austria-Hungary versus the Entente Powers of France, Great Britain, Russia and Serbia), a new nationalist government found an opportunity to "Turkify" their territories and the Armenians made easy targets. Aside from the years' long, simmering distrust, the "outsiders" also made convenient scapegoats when the Ottoman army faced heavy losses. Armenian "traitors" would sometimes be blamed, even while many remained loyal to the Ottoman Turkey side and fought bravely.

The situation deteriorated quickly. Armenian soldiers were disarmed and sent to forced labor.

Armenian intellectuals and influential members of the community were rounded up, some deported or killed. Healthy males became targets because they were potential threats. Some of these targets were forced into arming themselves and actively resisting, thus actualizing what the Ottoman Turks feared would happen. Even theoretically non-threatening Armenians – women, children, other civilians – suffered from maltreatment that would later be considered acts of genocide by many nations. There was seizure of property, confiscation of children for conversion, detention, slavery, rape, and brutal killings that reportedly included desert death marches, burning and even crucifixion.

By the time the atrocities – the deliberate, systemic and state sponsorship character of which is still being denied and debated – ended, the toll was staggering. Of two million Armenians estimated to have resided in the Ottoman Empire before the crimes against them started around 1915, less than half a million were left by 1922. Records can be confusing amidst the war and porous borders of the time, but deaths from the "Armenian Genocide" is estimated to fall within the range of 600,000 to 1.5 million. After the First World War and the Genocide, the country would also be affected by the fall of the Russian Empire and the rise of Soviet Russia.

Spared from all of these hardships was 17-year-old Tatos Kardashian, who headed to the United States on the heels of his parents in 1913; and the woman who would become his wife in Los Angeles, Hamas Shakarian. They started a waste disposal business and raise a family. Their son, Arthur Kardashian, married Helen Arakelian. Like Arthur, she was an American-born child of people who had left Armenia before the country's succession of tragedies.

Arthur and Helen were the parents of Robert Kardashian, whom we all know as the first standard bearer of the family name in the age of modern celebrity, and father to television and pop culture's most famous siblings.

The Kardashians of Los Angeles eventually made their fortune in the meatpacking business, which became one of the state's largest. But like many big businesses, it found itself under heavy government scrutiny. They ran afoul of investigators over accusations of bribery and corruption. One of Arthur and Helen's sons, Thomas, then a manager, took the biggest hit in the family (though he wouldn't get any jail time, and would eventually get a government pardon decades later). Their other son, Robert, was busy in pursuit of a career in law and business and was not implicated.

Kris' First True Love. Robert had a business administration degree from the University of Southern California, and a law degree from the University of San Diego. These credentials served him well in the careers he pursued, initially as a lawyer and afterwards in a slew of successful business ventures. He ran a trade publication, *Radio & Records*, and had a music video company and a frozen yoghurt shop. His net worth was estimated to be in the tens of millions of dollars.

But as was earlier mentioned, just because he had a lot of money did not mean he was reckless with them. He reportedly held off on indulgences for Kris when she was his girlfriend, but she was said to have made up for lost time by living extravagantly when she became his wife. She was so extravagant that some people would question her motives for marrying Robert and would even brand her a gold-digger. Not that he did not have his own quirks. Robert was reportedly eager for a housewife fitting to his values and lifestyle and towards that end, he was not subtle about molding his high school-educated, much younger wife into that ideal image. He is said to have required Kris to read various self-help references on domestic life, and expected her to be conversant with him on her learnings. Some say he veered toward being controlling or dominant, while others say he just wanted his younger wife to be more knowledgeable. Either way, Kris was always a quick study with plenty of charms, and she was able to channel the resources she had at her disposal into becoming a delightful Beverly Hills hostess. Their home was always a fun place to be.

They were a good-looking couple of power and means, and their life only seemed to be sweeter with the prompt arrival of beautiful children. Kourtney was born in 1979 and she was quickly followed by Kim in 1980. Home for the Kardashian girls and their parents was a Beverly Hills estate with a swimming pool and tennis courts. The fancy address, coupled with Kris' homemaking skills and Robert's connections, made their home the place to party for a lot of famous names and faces. Among the celebrities who have gathered here were Grammy winner, Lionel Richie; boxing champ, Sugar Ray Leonard; and Heisman Trophy winner and media personality, O.J. Simpson. The Kardashian home was also a pit stop for plenty of young family friends or classmates before they became famous later in their lives – Michael Jackson's nephew, T.J. Jackson; Rod Stewart's daughter, Kimberly; Lionel Richie's daughter, Nicole; and of course, reality TV star, pop culture phenomenon and Hilton hotels socialite, Paris Hilton. Aside from the glittering guests, the house had helpers and nannies for upkeep, and the siblings attended exclusive schools. Vacations for the family meant Palm Springs, or jaunts to Colorado for skiing and stops also included Hawaii and Mexico.

It was a lavish material life, but also a spiritual one. Robert was devout. He would post symbols of his faith on his beloved fancy car and go to services and bible study with his wife. He prayed daily and before meals. He had a Bible he held dear and would often read from, and he shared his faith and beliefs with his children.

In 1984, Kourtney and Kim were followed by another sister, Khloe. This was a controversial birth that would be shrouded in parentage questions for decades. Because beneath all of the trappings they had in their lives, Kris and Robert were not in the best of terms. And it was said that the increasingly restless Kris may have been intimate with someone else around the time Khloe was conceived.

Khloe's distinctly different appearance from her other siblings only served to feed the fire of rumors, some of which are truly on the wild side. Some people claim Robert Kardashian himself told them that he had doubted their third daughter's parentage – but he loved his daughter just the same (indeed, Khloe would be particularly hard hit by his death from cancer in 2003). A number of theories swirl around the identity of her real biological father – was she a product of indiscretion between some of the men who were in the Kardashian family's close circles, like Robert's good friend and business partner, O.J. Simpson, or Kris' hairdresser, Alex Roldan, or friend Lionel Richie? Or perhaps the real answer is the most uncontroversial one – for Khloe is actually described as looking pretty much like her dad's mother, Helen. What underlies all of these theories though, is that Kris had been unfaithful during her marriage with Robert. What we do not know, is if any of these indiscretions resulted in a child.

The marriage staggered along for a little while longer, and the couple would even have a fourth baby, their only son, Robert Jr. in 1987. But the union was not to last much longer after that.

Kris' Biggest Regret. Kris had often been vocal about her admiration for her late, first, ex-husband. She credited him and her exposure to the smart, wealthy and powerful circles he tended to move around in, for her own business acumen. She was also open about considering the mistakes she had made in her first marriage as amongst the biggest regrets of her life. Because some years into their marriage, the young mother and Beverly Hills' hot, hostess housewife was getting bored and restless. Kris played hard, partying and drinking and staying out until the wee hours of the morning. It may have been due to her age; she had settled down in her early 20s and had 4 children before she was in her mid-30s, and perhaps she wanted to see what of life she may have missed out on. She also may have been too young to understand the ups and downs of a long-running marriage, and wanted to explore other options.

One man's name would often be mentioned in reference to this tough stage of the Kardashians' troubled marriage. Soccer player, Todd Waterman, was ten years younger than Mrs. Kardashian. He and

Kris were reportedly caught by Robert several times. Kris' infidelity eventually led to their 1991 divorce and she would always regret it.

The dissolution of their parents' marriage was a heartbreaker for the otherwise privileged Kardashian kids, but life went on and all too soon, there was family anew and by many accounts, it was also a loving one. Before her divorce with Robert was even finalized, Kris was already in a serious relationship with iconic, Olympic gold medalist Bruce Jenner - a handsome, celebrated athlete who achieved legendary status decades earlier after a record-setting, Soviet-beating performance at the 1976 games in Canada. They married just a handful of weeks following the end of her marriage to Robert Kardashian, and just a few months after they were set up on a blind date.

Robert and Kris Kardashian's marriage may have come to an end, but the ex-couple maintained a co-parenting relationship for the sake of the four children they shared and loved. Kris' first and second husbands were even said to have gotten along, and the kids split their time between their parents' homes.

Ironically, the greatest strain their post-marriage relationship would suffer was actually not due to contentious relations with each other. Robert's best friend and business partner, the football hero and media personality, O.J. Simpson, was accused of murdering his ex-wife Nicole – one of Kris' best friends. The Kardashian exes inevitably found themselves on opposite sides of the courtroom drama that would absorb the entire United States, and change the dynamics of modern celebrity ever after.

The Trial of the Century. In June, 1994, O.J. Simpson was one of the people under suspicion of a brutal double-murder – the stabbing deaths of his ex-wife, Nicole Brown Simpson and her friend, Ronald Goldman. "The Juice," as O.J. was known, was a beloved African American sports figure who was the consummate celebrity. After his glory days as an athlete, he was a businessman, actor and television personality. The accusations levied against him would have made the murder case sensational on its own, but the case seemed to encapsulate the zeitgeist too, and so a number of other factors contributed to making the case all but a national obsession.

When the case began, memories were still fresh on the testy race relations with law enforcement from the Rodney King incident and the Los Angeles riots. The time was also the dawn of 24/7 media coverage, that was able to make quasi-celebrities of even "normal" people. Suddenly, one could be a private civilian and have an army of press camped outside one's house (as Robert Kardashian lamented at the conclusion of the Simpson court proceedings). There was now rapt interest and available technology and press presence that made information on virtually anyone involved in the trial available to the public. The judge had also allowed cameras into the courtroom. Thus, anyone who was interested the proceedings had both information access and inevitably, an opinion.

The court proceedings and its revolving door of a truly colorful cast of characters (cue the unforgettably named, Kato Kaelin), only fed the public's hunger for more information. But even before the trial began, O.J. himself fed the flames when he apparently tried to evade impending arrest by leading the police on an ill-conceived white Ford Bronco police chase (televised, of course).

This was just days after the murder, and the home he had been sheltering in prior to the infamous drive? His best friend, Robert Kardashian's. It was also Robert who read before hundreds of media a letter from O.J., which was initially believed to be a suicide note.

Robert Kardashian continued to be a prominent presence on O.J.'s side on his journey to the "not guilty" verdict he would eventually be granted by the legal system. Robert, whose lawyer's license had long lapsed as he focused more on becoming a businessman, reactivated it so that he could be present whenever his accused friend needed him. Thus, Kardashian became a fixture on the defense table over the course of the trial in 1995. He wasn't just there for decoration or moral support, however; he functioned almost like a liaison between

O.J. and his pricey, "Dream Team" of lawyers, a kind of compass for O.J.'s needs and wants.

Kardashian's role in O.J.'s case would be tarnished by rumors of a far more nefarious nature, however, and these rumors would trail him (and his family) for decades to come. He had apparently brought out a piece of Louis Vuitton luggage from O.J.'s house after the murders. Some posit it may have contained vital evidence that could have sunk the case, perhaps even the murder weapon that had not been found. Some even theorize that it's this depth of involvement that necessitated him to reactivate his legal license and stand by his friend as an attorney, therefore binding him to silence and confidentiality.

Attempts have been made in the ensuing years to set the record straight. Kardashian had spoken of the un-meaningful contents of the bag in a 1996 interview. But when the hit television series, *The People v. O.J. Simpson: American Crime Story*, brought the issue back into the public consciousness in 2016 – over two decades after the trial! –

Kardashian's now ultra-famous second daughter, Kim Kardashian-West, still found herself dispelling rumors.

If the loyal Robert was alleged to have had a hand in the murder weapon though, his ex-wife Kris, who had some knowledge of Nicole's troubles from an allegedly jealous and temperamental O.J., was also so close to the case that she may have actually been with Nicole when the slain woman bought history's most famous pair of gloves – the bloody pair that O.J. memorably tried on in the courtroom, to show that "*If the glove doesn't fit, you must acquit.*" The two women had purchased a pair of leather gloves (which may or may not have been the gloves in question) for O.J. in New York together.

Robert was loyal and stood by O.J. while Kris was also present for the trials (at times seated with the slain Nicole's family), even if she was already pregnant with her first child by Bruce Jenner (whom they eventually named Kendall Nicole). Kris would later explain that the respect she and Robert had for each other and the fact that they had children together, helped them weather having such contrasting loyalties and opinions regarding their two dear friends.

Intriguingly, it was Robert's friendship with O.J. that eventually soured. Two instances may have spurred the distance between the two men – over the years since the acquittal, Kardashian was candid about his own doubts about the case, and he had also participated in a book about the trial that O.J. felot was inappropriate.

A Lasting Legacy. At the end of this "Trial of the Century," Robert Kardashian – successful businessman but otherwise private citizen – had become a household name. He married a couple of times after Kris but had no other children. Unfortunately he wouldn't live to see his first wife and kids conquering the worlds of business and celebrity. He received a stage IV esophageal cancer diagnosis in 2003 and weeks later, at the age of 59, he passed away. His wife by then, Ellen Pierson, was someone he married shortly before his death, though they have been together for many years prior. Her relationship with the Kardashian kids and Robert's ex-wife, Kris, however, is unfortunate and litigious (questions were raised about his will and possessions, and the family found issue with the last Mrs. Robert Kardashian Sr.'s release of entries from their dad's diary, as well as her comments on Khloe's parentage).

Kris and the kids would always be all praises for Robert himself though. They are very open with their admiration for the man who first shone a light on their name and raised his family – in a way, including his younger wife – to work hard and value each other.

III. Mrs. Bruce Jenner

The fetching former Mrs. Robert Kardashian would capture the heart of another achiever.

William Bruce Jenner was born in New York on the 28th of October, 1949. He was said to be dyslexic as a youth, but had great aptitude for sports including basketball, football, water skiing and track. His football prowess was enough for a scholarship to college in Iowa, but an injury to his knee had him shifting his energies to track and field. It was a fortuitous injury and decision. Domination of the sport would come for the handsome, hard-working Bruce Jenner quickly.

Just a few years into his time in the sport, he placed third in Olympic trials, and had a respectable showing at the Summer Olympics in Munich in 1972. While there though, he witnessed the domination of Soviet athlete (and consequently, America's rival),

Mykola Avilov who ended up bringing home the gold.

He resolved to work harder, with a daily regime including 6-8 hours of training every day pretty much until the 1976 Olympic Games in Canada. He dominated the competitive road on the way to the Olympics and when he finally got there, he won the gold, set a world record, and became a sporting icon. The latter came about not just because he had succeeded in taking the crown from the Soviets, but also because he created an unforgettable Olympic moment that many athletes would follow afterwards. He celebrated bearing an American flag that a fan had run up to give him. Everyone loved it, and loved him.

Bruce Jenner cashed in on his newfound fame as one of the greatest athletes in the world (not a superfluous claim, since there are ten track and field events in a decathlon). But beyond the realm of sports, he became a beloved American celebrity, whose handsome likeness would appear on Wheaties boxes, as well as in other endorsements for companies like Minolta and Tropicana. He guest starred in television shows, appeared in films and did paid speaking engagements. He graced the covers of top-of-the-line magazines like *Sports Illustrated* and *GQ*.

At the height of his renown, Bruce Jenner was legendary. By the time he got together with Kris in the 1990s though, the opportunities no longer came like they used to. He was still a recognizable figure – he was into racing and had some speaking engagements, but it was far from the days of his Olympic glory. He'd been married twice and had children by them. He also reportedly did not have a lot of funds saved up in the bank.

Kris did not have much to offer in the way of finances herself. Robert Kardashian had cut her off. In an interview, she described how her credit cards ceased to work, and how she didn't even have the ability to pay for a tomato. But Bruce and Kris were in love. They were set up on a date by common friends and married a few months later. They were going to find a way to make things work.

One of the things they actively worked on was to make sure their children would have a happy and loving family life. Kris, Bruce and Robert cooperated and got along for them. Robert had frequent and regular access to Kourtney, Kim, Khloe and Rob. Next, Kris started her first project as a manager: her new husband.

A decade spent married to a savvy lawyer and businessman and walking in his brilliant circles, had given Kris a sense for capitalizing on an opportunity… and in Bruce Jenner, she saw blazing potential. Jenner was a gifted speaker with an amazing story to tell, and his new wife set about helping him tell his tale to a wider audience and be paid handsomely for it.

Kris put together professional press kits on Bruce and sent them out strategically, in a bid to land him more speaking engagements. The callbacks came, but Kris was just beginning. She helped keep Bruce in the public eye – in fitness infomercials, in talk shows, events and game shows. It was almost chicken-and-egg, how she cultivated his fame toward more opportunities, and these opportunities into more fame, and so on. Bruce thrived as the revived star, and Kris thrived as kingmaker, a role she would play pretty much to perfection ever afterwards. She is widely credited for Bruce Jenner's career revival. She in turn, would credit her late first husband for the business acumen that had rubbed off on her, as well as for her exposure to his networks.

Caitlyn Jenner Rising. Bruce Jenner had a great gig as a retired Olympian, but he was only the warning shot in Mrs. Kris Jenner's expansive arsenal for world domination. They had four Kardashian kids and two Jenner girls of their own, Kendall and Kylie (born in 1995 and 1997, respectively), who were all growing up to be beautiful, fun and simply *fascinating*. They were practically characters on a television show…

If Bruce was the warning shot, Kris' second daughter by Robert Kardashian, Kim, was the first salvo and she was a hit. She already had exposure to celebrity on the periphery of early reality TV trailblazer and pop culture phenom, Paris Hilton's fame. When Kim became the stunning subject of a leaked sex tape and a multi-million-dollar settlement, she became famous on her own right. She was also a beauty unconventional for the cookie-cutter waifs of the time. Celebrity and opportunity quickly came knocking on her door.

But Kris really went nuclear when she pitched her blended family as the subject of a reality TV show for Ryan Seacrest Productions and E!. When they were picked up, it reportedly wasn't because of audiences expected to be drawn in by Kim's sexy persona; it was on account of the colorful family's crazy authenticity and obvious affection for each other.

The show aired in 2007 and was quickly picked up for another season. And another and another and another… as of this writing in 2018, *Keeping Up with the Kardashians* is still running, and had already spawned spin-offs and specials aplenty over the years.

In the earlier seasons, Bruce Jenner tended to look like the semi-retired, leisurely, grounded and somewhat conservative *paterfamilias* who generally indulged the madness of being in an occasionally overbearing family. But in a stunning turn of events that is stranger than fiction, something no one could have been able to make up, Bruce threw everyone a curveball.

He was in his 60s and married over 20 years with Kris. They were living with a scandalous amount of means thanks to their long-running hit show, its collection of spin-offs, and other paid opportunities that came with being a business savvy modern celebrity. Few people would have anticipated a drastic change in circumstances for the oldest couple of the crew.

But Bruce had long identified as a woman, and wanted a chance to pursue the life she felt she was meant to have. She had gender identity issues since childhood, sneaking around in her mother and sister's clothing. She lived in a more restrictive time and was herself a conservative, so she grappled with what it all meant. She reportedly discussed her struggles with her first spouse, her college sweetheart

Chrystie Crownover, with whom she was married from 1972 to 1981 and with whom she shares two kids. They tried to make things work, and Chrystie never cited her spouse's gender identity as a reason for their split. Chrystie also kept her spouse's secret to herself, opening up publicly about the precious secret only when Bruce herself finally spoke up about it in 2015. Chrystie was very supportive of her former spouse.

Bruce's second wife, Linda Thompson is a beautiful multi-hyphenate with a string of claims to fame; she is an actress – model - Elvis Presley's ex – former beauty queen - TV personality – columnist – activist / philanthropist - and multi-award-winning songwriter. They met at a celebrity charity tennis tournament and their friendship soon blossomed into a romance that brought them down the aisle in 1981. The marriage yielded two kids too. They had a good family life inclusive of Bruce's children with Chrystie. But Bruce's identity struggles eventually made its way into their idyllic home life. They tried to work together and find ways of letting Bruce live as her authentic self while keeping Linda's sense of home and family, but they eventually divorced in 1984.

In both his previous marriages, Bruce had been somewhat open of her gender identity issues with her spouses. It hadn't been smooth sailing and still ended in divorce, but both ex-wives had also been protective of Bruce's struggles, opening up about them only when she herself proved ready decades later. Her marriage and post-divorce relationship with her third wife, Kris, would unfortunately be more contentious for many reasons. They couldn't even agree on precisely how much Kris knew of Bruce's struggles and when she knew it.

By one account, Bruce had already been in initial forms of transition after her second divorce, such that Kris may have spotted feminine changes in Bruce's body when they met – hair removal, some breasts. By another account, Bruce was open about taking hormones, but Kris misunderstood them to be in the context of his past athletic life. In another account, Bruce was honest but not fully, underplaying her gender identity issues. By yet another account, Kris was aware of her spouse's tendencies but was passively accepting of them. It is still unknown what Kris knew and when she knew it or the precise impetus for the end of their marriage. Bruce would memorably say to *Vanity Fair* that the ending was due less to gender and more from how she was treated.

Either way, after more than two decades of being together, they announced their separation in 2013. They did the usual statements about continuing friendship, and finalized their divorce in 2014. Amidst all of this, there were rumors of Bruce's transition but both she and Kris kept quiet on the issue. Bruce chose to make her truth known in as much of a controlled way as a public figure of her status could, via a groundbreaking interview with Diane Sawyer in April, 2015. It was followed by an outpouring of support from his family, Kardashian kids and ex-wife Kris included.

While Kris kept up a graceful stance of strength and support, however, she also harbored private pains. She was anguished that she had cherished memories of a past life that seemed not to have been authentic after all. But still, ever the professional, she kept a strong face as long as she could… until some statements from Bruce threw here resolve to stay positive and civil out the window.

Bruce revealed herself as Caitlyn in the June, 2015, issue of *Vanity Fair*, where she was featured in all her glamorous glory on the cover. But she also revealed negative feelings about what she perceived as Kris' deteriorated tolerance and poor treatment of her over time. Statements like these proved naturally upsetting to the family matriarch, whose daughters also took exception with the negative portrayal of their beloved mother. The exes seemed to be on a truce in the latter quarter of the year though, and were spotted together in support of their now-grown supermodel daughter, the stunning Kendall, as she strutted her stuff at the Victoria's Secret Fashion Show in New York. But the fragile armistice would not survive the storm of 2017, which was when Caitlyn's memoir, *The Secrets of My Life*, was released. The Kardashian family again found issue with not only some of its negativity, but also considered some of the entries untruthful.

The relationship, while civil on behalf of their children, Kendall and Kylie (who maintain a relationship with Caitlyn even if the older girls have not been fully able to), unfortunately remains frosty as of this writing (September, 2018).

IV. "Momager"

Caitlyn Jenner may have harbored ill feelings of her ex-spouse, Kris, but no one could find fault with how shrewd Kris was in business, and how well everyone in the Kardashian-Jenner brood made bank because of what she started.

Caitlyn, for example, is said to be worth around $100 million from television paychecks via *Keeping Up with the Kardashians* and her own show, *I Am Cait*, as well as from her memoir. When she isn't busy with transition, being a parent, and dealing with the Kardashian fallout from her controversial claims, Caitlyn busies herself with her new community. Given her public persona, she carries the hopes of the ostracized and disadvantaged in the LGBTQ+ sectors, that she would be instrumental in pushing for their better acceptance in society. Her conservative-leaning politics have been a disappointment to many, but it is all a work-in-progress.

In the meantime, Kris has an empire to run and grow. She is said to wake up as early as 5 am for brainstorming or work in her home office. She is also the often the first phone call to make in the event of a disaster, which can come from any corner because she has six famous kids each with their own careers. She also somehow found time to fall in love again.

The Growth of an Empire. Kris Jenner turned what could have been fifteen minutes of fame into over fifteen years of fortune for herself and her family. She had a vision to pursue, the courage to try, and the grit to just keep going. The Kardashians were relentless, going after every opportunity especially in the early years. That level of tenacity seemed to run in the blood, and traces of it could be spotted in pretty much each member of the family.

Kim Kardashian and her infamous sex tape kicked things off in some ways, but she was much more than that. The second child of Kris and Robert was beautiful in a rich, exotic, altogether original way, but more than that, she seemed to have her parents' smarts and guts. She married young and divorced young. She kept the networks she had gleaned from her privileged upbringing and parlayed it not only into work as a wardrobe organizer / personal shopper / stylist to the stars – it also got her little cameos in shows like Paris Hilton's *The Simple Life*; took her to red carpet events; eventually allowed her to open a fashion-related business venture, the high-end fashion store DASH in partnership with her sisters; and of course, got her a famous boyfriend… with whom she ended up featured in a sex tape.

The video was released by an entertainment company with initial resistance from the family, but Kim eventually settled and reportedly earned millions from it. The same year it came out, *Keeping Up with the Kardashians* first aired on E!, and Kim and her family would only become more famous and more wealthy from there.

Keeping Up with the Kardashians. Contrary to popular belief, the family did not bag a TV deal because of their gorgeous sister's sex tape. Media personality and emergent entertainment power player, Ryan Seacrest, was apparently on the lookout for a show not unlike the phenomenal *The Osbournes*, and was stirred to give the family a try after Kris Jenner made a pitch. What he saw – and what the powers-that-be over in *E!* eventually saw - was the family's chemistry, individual charisma, and genuine affection for each other. Over the years, they kept to that winning formula. *KUWTK* was about a crazy but loving family who, in spite of fame and fortune and the occasional staged situation, somehow seemed grounded and authentic in their reactions and love.

Going Beyond Television. *KUWTK* has been going on for over a decade, would span nine spin-off shows, and air in over 150 countries. It would form a chunk of each family member's paycheck, but not the entirety of it. This family after all, has figured out their own ways of channeling their fame into other business ventures. TV paychecks are in short, only a small slice of their total revenue stream. They do other projects both individually and collectively. Kim, older sister Kourtney and younger sister Khloe, for example, are the main forces behind the founding and expansion of their DASH stores. Kim has also appeared in movies and tried her hand in the music scene (not successfully, however).

Like many celebrities, members of the family certainly did and continue to do their share of endorsements and events, for which they are paid handsomely. Kim, for example, has lent her name and likeness to a workout video on DVD. She also did social media for a morning sickness pill. She had appeared in a Carl's Jr. commercial, an ad for T-Mobile and spoke for Midori, as well as (the ill-fated) Sketchers Shape-Ups and a diet product called QuickTrim. The sisters have also appeared for Calvin Klein and Balmain.

But traditional endorsements weren't the bulk of the revenue stream either. They did co-branding initiatives and collaborations with established companies in the making and marketing of products. They've worked with Sears, Kohls, PacSun, nail polish by OPI, Silly Bandz, and lines of fragrances (Kim, for example, had released four over the years!). Kim in particular, has also gotten royalties from the video game, *Kim Kardashian: Hollywood*, and a paid emoji pack called *Kimojis*.

But again, putting together TV paychecks, celebrity endorsements (traditional or social media), and royalties from collaborations still will not capture the full breadth of the Kardashian money-making machine… for the Kardashian-Jenner girls seemed to have the entrepreneurial spirit of the Campbell ladies, and they would do just what their mother Kris, grandmother M.J. and great-grandmother Ethyl did, but with a modern, digital spin…

They were early adapters on social media platforms like Twitter, Instagram and Snapchat and as of this writing, the family has a combined social media following to the tune of about 700 million people – a powerful voice that would not only allow them to bag even more endorsements, but also allow them to build and promote businesses of their own.

Kim would found the lucrative KKW Beauty cosmetics line in 2017, anchored on a contour kit but since expanding to other makeup. It quickly brought in $100 million in revenues, for a business that had minimal fixed costs – outsourced manufacturing and packaging and sales fulfillment, and low-cost marketing from using her own social media meant a hefty bottom-line. Her youngest sister Kylie would be an even bigger success in this model, founding a cosmetics company, 100% self-owned, selling hundreds of millions worth of make-up, pouting all the way to a net worth said to be in the realm of $900 million – and counting.

Theoretically, the success of children are reflective of their parents. But beyond theory, Kris Jenner actually manages and derives fees from many of her children's money-making activities and has direct influence in many of their affairs. Thus, to list her children's successes are to describe the feathers on this proud "momager's" cap:

Kim Kardashian, thanks to TV paychecks, endorsements, royalties, and businesses like KKW is said to have a net worth somewhere in the $350 million-level.

Kourtney Kardashian, the eldest daughter of Robert and Kris, has an estimated net worth of $35 million. She was the first Kardashian on reality TV (she had appeared on *Cattle Drive* and reportedly donated her earnings to charity), and the first among them to be involved in the retail business; she helped found and run DASH, and also worked with Kris in a children's store. Her millions, however, came from her television paychecks (via *KUWTK* and her involvement in a number of spin-offs); and the occasional celebrity endorsement and collaborations.

Khloe Kardashian, their third child, was practically made for TV with her fun, spontaneous and bubbly personality. It should be of no surprise then that she is able to find engagements beyond the family TV show. Her past projects include *X-Factor*, *Kocktails with Khloe* and *Revenge Body with Khloe Kardashian*. She was also on a season of *Celebrity Apprentice*. Thus, she made bank from *KUWTK*, several of its spin-offs, other television and radio hosting gigs, celebrity endorsements and collaborations, and of course, her own business too. Aside from DASH with her sisters, she and a partner launched a size-inclusive fashion line called Good

American, which reportedly made a $1million in sales on the first day it was launched in 2016. Her estimated net worth? $40 million.

Robert Kardashian Jr. Even the Kardashians' reluctant celebrity son is making bank. Kris and Robert's fourth child and only son, who took his esteemed father's name, has been an uneasy presence in the spotlight. He has shown signs of low self-esteem stemming from heavy weight gain, and had a period of poor productivity and not wanting to be seen and judged in public. Most recently, he was part of a troubled relationship, which is ironically the one thing the otherwise reclusive star is vocal about. And yet his net worth is still estimated at $10 million, from his TV paychecks (via *KUTWK* and the spinoff, *Rob & Chyna*) and his sock business, Arthur George. He'd previously also done *Dancing With the Stars* in 2011.

Kendall Jenner, Kris's first child by Bruce, grew up before the public eye. She was a tween when the show first aired but has since become one of the family's most recognizable faces. Her stunning beauty has graced the campaigns and runways of many a high fashion brand, and her acceptance in these tight circles is one of the proofs that the family has gone beyond guilty pleasure TV and kitschy capitalist opportunism - they have earned high fashion credibility. She is said to be worth of some $18 million, derived from her TV paychecks (she is the only Kardashian-Jenner sibling who has not yet featured in a spin-off though), and from being one of the highest paid working models in the fashion industry. She has been walking for famous runways since 2014, when she made a splash for Marc Jacobs. She is the face of Estee Lauder, had featured in edgy Calvin Klein campaigns, and had done work for Balmain, Chanel, Dolce & Gabbana, Fendi, Givenchy and Victoria's Secret. She is one of fashion's current It Girls, and has been on the cover of *the* American *Vogue's* September issue. She also runs a fashion line with younger sister Kylie, appropriately called, Kendall + Kylie.

Kylie Jenner, the youngest among the Kardashian-Jenner kids and the second of two children by Kris and Bruce, took America by surprise when she appeared on the cover of the iconic *Forbes* Magazine. The twenty-one-year-old's estimated net worth? $900 million, thanks mostly to a thriving cosmetics business expanded from lip kits, estimated to be worth $800 million. The rest comes from *KUWTK* and the spin-off, *Life of Kylie* paychecks, plus endorsements, and her clothing line with Kendall. She was only around nine years old when *KUWTK* started filming and airing in 2007! She sold lip kits in 2015 to runaway success and launched Kylie Cosmetics in 2016, which eventually went on to sell hundreds of millions of dollars' worth of cosmetics at minimal operating costs of a few employees; outsourced production, packaging and sales; essentially cost-free and highly targeted marketing efforts from her own expansive social media reach; and of course, help from the financial and business management of her mama, Kris.

V. The Next Frontier

We know that the Kardashians are able to leverage their fame to make money. But how is it that they are able to stay so famous and relevant? With so many exciting members of the same family each with compelling individual struggles… it is actually a wonder how they are able to simplify and keep a coherent and understandable storyline! It seems the Kardashian-Jenners are always on the cusp of something exciting, both for the good and the bad of it.

Kim Kardashian, for example, was absolutely compelling in her disastrous 2010 romance with NBA basketball player, Kris Humphries. Their divorce took much longer than their famously 72-day marriage. Their wedding was picture perfect (and drew the show's highest ratings). The union on the other hand, was later to be revealed as a regrettable mess. Kim has since married and raised kids with genius rap superstar and fashion icon, Kanye West. They have three beautiful kids, North, Saint and Chicago. Kanye is more private and is evasive on the reality TV show, but their union gave Kim a more polished persona with street cred in high fashion circles because her husband is a known tastemaker. The couple stays in the news due to their work, Kanye's controversial politics and mental health, and the seemingly ever-present rumors of trouble in paradise.

As for the other Kardashian-Jenners…

Kourtney, long-enthralled by Scott Disick, the father of her three children, Mason, Penelope and Reign, also has an interesting "storyline" of finding love anew after almost a decade of troubled partnership with Scott, whose struggles with the party life have been a well-documented and recurring theme on *KUWTK* for years. She is trying to be a hands-on mom and a celebrity at the same time, and her priorities, especially when it comes to managing her time, sometimes puts her in conflict with her workaholic family. She recently exited a relationship with the model and former boxer, Younes Bandjima, who is said to be 14 years younger than her.

Khloe's love life is just as filled with ups and downs. A whirlwind romance with NBA player Lamar Odom resulted in a marriage that also came to a sad end, as his troubled personality adversely affected their union. Khloe, religious and loyal, had to find ways of reconciling her vows to her husband and her own happiness and welfare. She was nevertheless stalwartly by his side when he was found unconscious in 2015 and helped him through his recovery. A romantic reconciliation was not in the cards however, and she went on to date other high-profile men, among them rapper French Montana and Houston Rockets star, James Harden. In 2016, she became linked to Tristan Thompson, with whom she would eventually have a child, True, in 2018 – even as Tristan's infidelity made the media rounds.

Also controversial was Rob's relationship with Blac Chyna, the mother of his child, Dream. Their rocky relationship was beset by accusations of cheating and abuse. Blac Chyna was also the ex of Kylie's former flame, the rapper Tyga. But it is with another rapper, Travis Scott, that Kylie would have her first child, Stromi.

The least entangled of the family, Kendall, wouldn't be exempt from her own troubles. A Pepsi ad she had starred in would be pulled within a day under a storm of protest over disrespect for the Black Lives Matter Movement. Kendall was also named in a palimony suit filed by the ex-girlfriend of her then-boyfriend, NBA star Blake Griffin. Griffin is just one of the famous romantic interests that have been linked to the young stunner. Among her famous exes is the pop superstar, Harry Styles.

This is an intricate tapestry of lives and at its center, trying to keep the family from unraveling while spinning a wider web of commitments and achievements is the "momager," Kris Jenner. At least she is able to pursue some romantic happiness for herself.

The last few years have seen her in the romantic company of handsome tour manager producer, Corey Gamble, who is more than 20 years her junior. Gamble, who is said to have worked with

Justin Bieber, is estimated to be worth an estimated $3 million himself. They met in August, 2014 in Spain at Riccardo Tisci's birthday bash, and have been together on and off since they started dating later that year.

Like many of the colorful men and women who had walked in and out of the Kardashian's lives, Gamble has appeared on the family show and has proven to be steadfast in spite of their occasional off moments. Rumors of a wedding are loud and frequent, but Kris expressed hesitations over walking down the aisle one more time after everything she has experienced.

Kris has the resources to be pretty much anything she wants to be at this point. She'd been Kris Houghton, Natalie Wood lookalike, teenager with stars and dollar signs in her big, beautiful eyes. She'd been Mrs. Robert Kardashian with Beverly Hills at her feet, and Mrs. Bruce Jenner, kingmaker. She tried to pursue a career on her own, as with her efforts in the 1990s as correspondent on the daytime talk show, *Mike & Maty*; and on her own short-lived show in the 2010s. But what she had always been was a mom, and she found the most success and perhaps the most fulfillment in building the other people she loves in her life. As "momager" she did not just build individual kings (or more precisely, queens!), she built empires.

And as her litany of achievements show, Kris Houghton Kardashian Jenner is self-0made, buty that is almost an understatement of what she has managed to do in her life. She isn't just self-made.

She made others.

35949554R00049

Made in the USA
San Bernardino, CA
16 May 2019